# Time for Peace

## Janet Ganguli

## Quaker Press
OF FRIENDS GENERAL CONFERENCE

PHILADELPHIA, PA

Copyright © Janet Ganguli 2003

First published in 1999 by Small World Publications, 31 Caxton End, Bourn, Cambridge CB3 7SS, UK

ISBN 1-888305-30-4

Printed in the United States of America

Front cover: One panel of hundreds from all over the world that made up the remarkable peace "Ribbon" draped around the Pentagon, Washington, D.C. (The U.S. version of Defence Ministry) in August 1985.

Back cover: The dove on the back cover is based on a 13th century mosaic showing how the desire for peace continues through the centuries. This image is currently displayed at the United Nations.

Original composition and design by Manan Ganguli, adapted for US publication by Quaker Press of FGC.


For more information about this title contact:
Quaker Press of Friends General Conference
1216 Arch Street 2B
Philadelphia, PA 19107

To order more copies of this publication or other Quaker titles call QuakerBooks of FGC at
1-800-966-4556 or on the world wide web at www.quakerbooks.org

# Contents

# *Acknowledgements*

Many people have helped me with the preparation of this book. I would particularly like to thank my brother, Martin Aitken, who helped improve the text and the Sir James Reckitt Charity which helped fund the production of the first edition. I would also like to thank Jan Melichar and Annie Bebington of the Peace Pledge Union, Lionel Trippett of the Campaign for Nuclear Disarmament, David Baker of the Gandhi Peace Foundation, Carol Rank of the Bradford Peace Museum, Virginia Albaneso of the Chicago Peace Museum, Professor Joseph Rotblat, Roger Rawlinson (author of *Larzac*), Albert Beale, Angie Zelter and Rowan Tilly.

**Picture Acknowledgements:**

Front cover: from 'The Ribbon'/Lark Books, USA, p. 64; banner produced by Victor Initiative for Peace, New York; photo/Julie Gelfand, reproduced with permission from Chicago Peace Museum • The Peace Museum, Chicago, IL, USA, p. 1 • John Searle-Barnes: p. 3 (First World War cemetery) • Yamahata: p. 3 (Nagasaki) • Panos Pictures: p. 4 • Scott Polar Research Institute: p. 5 (right) • OIPP/J. Puusa: p. 5 (left) • War Resisters League Peace Calendar (1998) / Ed Hedemann: p. 10, Minora Aoke: p. 28 (left) • Ethelwyn Best/'Pierre Ceresole—Passionate Peacemaker': p. 12 • Religious Society of Friends in Britain: p. 13, 19 and 36 (above) • Daniele Lamarche: p. 15 • Joe Payne/Jonathon Cape: p. 16 • Hulton Picture Library: p. 18 (left) • Judges postcards Ltd, Hastings (tel. 01424 420919): p. 18 (right) • Commonweal Collection: p. 23 • Popperfoto: p. 23 (below) and 39 • 'Norwegian Diary'/Friends Peace and International Relations Committee: p. 24 • Czech News Agency/CTK: p. 25 • Magnum photos: p. 28 (right) • Ricarda Steinbrecher: p. 31 • Ed Barber, 'Peace Moves'/Hogarth Press: p. 32 (left) and 58 • Greenpeace: p. 32 (right) • Campaign for Nuclear Disarmament: p. 34 • Mayibuye Centre Photo Library/University of the Western Cape: p. 36 (right) • National Gandhi Museum, New Delhi: p. 37 • Corbis/Bettmann: p. 38 (right) • The Nobel Foundation: p. 38 (Ossietzky), 41 (Sakharov and Nobel medals) • Peace People: p. 40 • Oregon Historical Society: p. 42 (Pauling) • Peace Pledge Union: p. 43 (war toy conversion) • Grass Roots House, Kochi, Japan: p. 45 • 'Songs for Peace'/CND: p. 44 • Back cover: adapted from 'Dove of Peace.'

Dear young readers,

Maybe you have heard in the news or from your parents and grandparents about the destruction and suffering of war.

Maybe sometimes you wonder why this happens and if it has to happen.

This book tells you a little about why wars take place and about all the different ways in which people are trying to prevent them. It shows you that wars do not have to happen. There is another way.

I hope that when you grow up the world will be a more peaceful and happier place.

October 1999

*A way of death*

*Cannot defend*

*A way of life*

*My worthy friend.*

*A day of strife*

*Could kill us all*

*If missiles fall.*

*A way of life*

*Cannot be led*

*If you are dead.*

Michael Aitken

# What Is Peace?

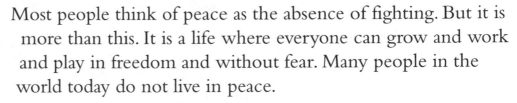

Most people think of peace as the absence of fighting. But it is more than this. It is a life where everyone can grow and work and play in freedom and without fear. Many people in the world today do not live in peace.

Wars are made by people. No other animal on earth fights each other and causes such destruction as we do. When other animals of the same kind fight each other, they seldom kill.

There were two terrible world wars in the 20th century. Since the end of World War II in 1945, there have been over 130 wars. In many parts of the world people are suffering the effects of war and long for peace.

In previous centuries soldiers fought battles. Nowadays it is not only the fighting men and women who lose their lives or become injured, it is mainly ordinary people in their homes including children. Some children have never known peace in their lifetime.

# Some Wars around the World

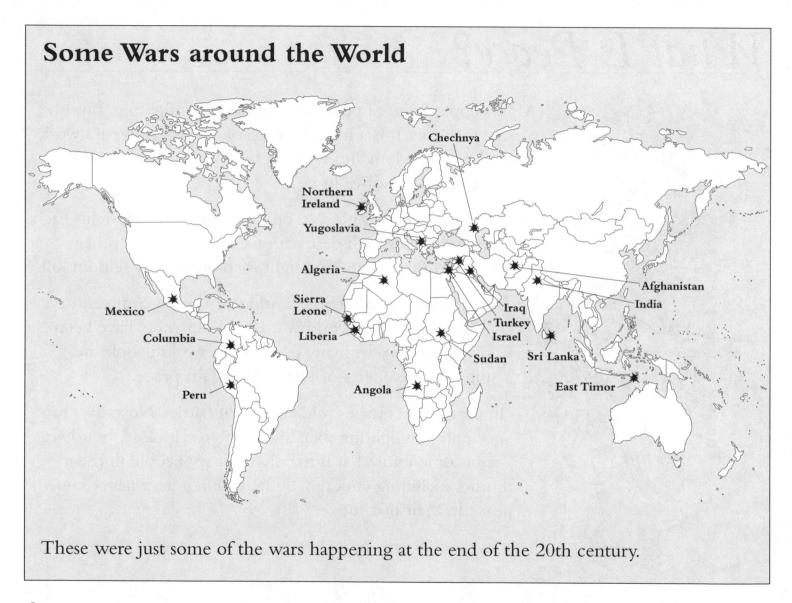

Chechnya

Northern Ireland

Yugoslavia

Algeria

Sierra Leone

Liberia

Mexico

Columbia

Peru

Angola

Sudan

Iraq

Turkey

Israel

Afghanistan

India

Sri Lanka

East Timor

These were just some of the wars happening at the end of the 20th century.

# The Effects of War

- Death and injury of loved ones.

- Destruction of homes, hospitals, schools, churches, historic buildings, factories.

- Hunger and starvation from the destruction of harvests and of the roads and bridges needed to transport food.

- Disease due to hunger and the destruction and pollution of water sources.

- Destruction of livestock, wildlife, trees and forests.

- Refugees: many people flee their homes in fear of their lives. They have no means of supporting themselves and are prey to hunger and disease. They also suffer mentally from what has happened to them.

**The effects of war continue for many, many years after the fighting has stopped.**

# All members of the human family

# Why Do Wars Happen?

## Human Groups

Although we are all human beings with the same kind of body and the same kind of feelings, we divide ourselves up into groups. We group ourselves according to our nationality, our language, our religion, our tribe, our colour and so on. This can be a good thing because it gives us a feeling of "belonging," of identity, of knowing who we are. But it also has dangers when we come to think that our "group" is better than another group or we feel bad because another group appear to think they are better than us.

One of the most important groups are national groups. National groups are very strong. From a young age we are encouraged to think of ourselves as belonging to a particular country, of being British or French or Russian and so on. The language and traditions we learn all help to reinforce this.

*The love of one's country is a splendid thing. But why should love stop at the border?*
— Pablo Casals (Spanish musician)

We are taught that patriotism is a good thing. To be patriotic means to love and serve your country. While we are taught to love and serve our country, so other children in other countries are taught to love and serve their country. This can mean following what the leaders of your country tell you to do rather than deciding for yourself if it is right or wrong.

All countries have leaders. They may be called president or prime minister or king and they have people in their country who support them although not all of them do.

## Power

Sometimes the leaders of countries are not content with the power and land and resources they have and they want more power and land. Many wars start because the leaders of a country want more power and more land.

It is the leaders of countries who decide to make war, not the ordinary people. Leaders work hard at making people think that the war is a good thing. They even tell lies to make them feel this way. They use words in a way that makes the people feel that another group of people is their enemy. The enemy are portrayed as bad people. But in fact they are ordinary people too. During World War II the Russians were our allies. After the war our leaders made them into our enemies.

> *Of course the people don't want war . . . it is the leaders of the country who determine the policy and it is always a simple matter to drag the people along.*
> — Hermann Goering (Hitler's deputy) on trial in Nuremburg

# Armed Forces

Almost every country has an army. In many countries young men have to serve in the armed forces for a certain length of time when they have finished their studies. In Britain and the United States this no longer happens. Instead we have a "professional" army and advertisements are shown encouraging young people to join up. Serving in the armed forces is made to look exciting.

**ARMY**
**BE THE BEST**

Most people do not want to kill other people. In everyday life, killing someone is a crime. If someone kills someone else on purpose, it is called 'murder.' Murder is the worst crime there is.

In the army this is turned upside down. The army actually teaches how to kill other people. The soldiers have rigorous physical training to make their bodies fit and strong. At the same time they are made to believe

*When people are trained from childhood, they can be trained to believe any kind of nonsense . . . that it is not sinful for soldiers to kill people at the wish of those in command.*

— Leo Tolstoy (Russian writer)

that to kill is necessary to defend your country and means you are patriotic and brave. Not to kill is to be weak and cowardly. Soldiers are taught not to think for themselves but to obey orders. They are encouraged to shut out the feelings and thoughts they would normally have about doing something so horrible as killing another human being. After a war, for many soldiers the feelings and thoughts they have been taught to try and shut out, come back. The feeling that they have done terrible things is always inside them and makes them very unhappy.

## Weapons

Nowadays many of the weapons used to kill people are very powerful. It is possible to kill thousands of people with just one bomb. There are enough bombs in the world to blow up the whole earth several times over. Many scientists spend their time inventing more effective ways of killing people and thousands of people earn their living by making weapons.

The people who sell weapons make a great deal of money. It is useful for these people to have enemies and wars in order to keep making money.

So we are always preparing for war and therefore making it more likely. When people have spent so much time and money making or buying weapons, they will surely want to use them one day.

Wars do not happen suddenly. Events take place over a period of time—weeks, months and often years which eventually lead to war. If we are to stop war, we have to take steps along the road to peace all the time. It is not possible to bring peace by hoping and wishing for peace while all the time taking steps toward war. It is not possible to bring peace through war because they are opposite things. Each war creates more suffering and hatred; one war leads to another. Some people at the time called World War I "the war to end all wars." But instead it led to World War II. Wars do not solve problems. They make more problems.

This sculpture of a large replica revolver with its barrel tied into a knot stands near the United Nations General Assembly Building in New York.

*Peace cannot be kept by force. It can only be achieved by understanding.*
— Albert Einstein (German scientist)

# The cost of war and preparation for war

Paying for an army, navy and airforce and all the equipment and weapons costs a great deal of money. For example the British Trident submarine system costs about £4 million every day ($6,652,635 US). This money could be used to help those who are poor, to provide better health care and schools. It could be used to improve and save lives.

Besides the huge waste of money, our preparations for war cause great harm in another way. The testing of nuclear weapons has led to the spread of radiation all over the world. Many people will die from cancer caused by this radiation.

*Every gun that is made, every warship launched, every rocket fired, signifies in a final sense a theft from those who hunger and are not fed, those who are cold and are not clothed.*

— Dwight D. Eisenhower (US President 1953–61)

# Building Peace

If life on earth is to go on, learning to work for peace is one of the most important things in the world today. There are many ways to work for peace.

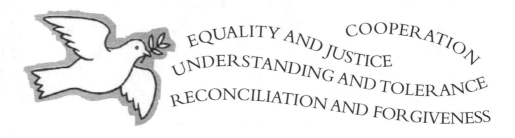

EQUALITY AND JUSTICE
COOPERATION
UNDERSTANDING AND TOLERANCE
RECONCILIATION AND FORGIVENESS

## Understanding and Tolerance

When we learn about and meet people from other national or religious groups, we can see that they are also people like us and we have nothing to fear from them. Then it is harder for the leaders of countries to make us think of them as our "enemies." Understanding does not mean you have to agree. Along with understanding we have to foster tolerance. Tolerance is when you accept that someone is different and you don't mind about it. Through tolerance we learn to see differences not as threat but as adding interest and richness to life. If everyone thought and acted in the same way, the world would be a very dull place!

Anglo-Russian Contacts (ARC) was formed in the 1960s at the height of the Cold War when we lived under the threat of war between the United States, Western Europe and Russia. ARC arranged visits and contacts between British and Russians.

# International Work Camps

Pierre Ceresole was a Swiss man who spent his life resisting war and working for peace. Several times he was sent to prison. After World War I, he set up an organisation called "Service Civil Internationale." He brought together French, Swiss, English and Germans (the people who had fought each other) to rebuild

Pierre Ceresole (1879–1945)

International work camp in a nature reserve in Holland.

together. International work camps continue to take place each year all over the world where young people from different countries learn about each other by living and working together.

# Cooperation

In the world we live in there is a great deal of competition all around us. From the time we are small we are encouraged to compete, to see who is best at something, who gets the highest marks and who can win.

But there is another way and that is to work together rather than against each other to achieve something. This way no one is left-out and there are no losers. Some people are good at one thing and some people at another thing: if we work together we can achieve more for everyone.

For example there is a traditional party game of musical chairs. Each time the music stops someone is 'out.' For the rest of the game they have to sit out and watch. One child will be the winner and the others feel a little sad or envious or even cheated. But it is very easy to arrange the game differently so that everyone can have fun. As the chairs or "islands" of paper become fewer and fewer so everyone has to help each other to stand on a smaller and smaller space when the music stops. Instead of ending up with one winner and many losers we end up with a great big hug!

**THE TWO MULES'**
A fable for the Nations

**CO-OPERATION
IS BETTER THAN CONFLICT**

# Equality and Justice

Unfortunately closeness and understanding do not always prevent war. Some of the most bitter wars have been fought between groups of people within one country. People who used to live peacefully side by side start killing each other: Jews and Arabs in Palestine, Hindus and Muslims in India, Tutsis and Hutus in Rwanda and Serbs and Muslims in Bosnia.

The leaders of one group seek to have more power than the other. Sometimes when things have not been going well in the country (there are not enough jobs for everyone or food has become very expensive) the leader of one group may blame it on the other group and turn his group against them. Sometimes one group uses their greater power to help themselves to a larger share of the country's wealth at the expense of the other group.

In Israel, which used to be called Palestine, there is a conflict between the Jews and the Arabs (Palestinians). Many Jews are coming into the country and taking over the land and villages where Arabs have lived and grown their crops for centuries. However, some of the Jewish people are trying to help the Palestinians. For example, week after week a group of Jewish women, who call themselves 'The Women in Black,' gather to protest about the taking of Arab land and the brutal treatment of the Arabs. They know that peace will come to this part of the world only when the Palestinians have their fair share of land and freedom.

# Without Justice There Is No Peace

So long as one group of people within a country is treated unfairly there can never be justice. Without justice there is no peace. Peace that lasts has to be based on justice for everyone.

To earn their living, some people pick things from garbage heaps, some people carry heavy loads for others. Many people live on the streets, they have no houses. Many children are not able to go to school, they work to help their family.

*True peace is not merely the absence of war, but it is the presence of justice.*

— Martin Luther King, Jr.

# Forgiveness and Reconciliation

Even when the fighting has stopped many people have suffered so much they are filled with pain, anger and bitterness. There is no peace in their hearts.

When someone hurts us, we may feel strongly that we want to hurt them back, to get 'revenge.' But so long as we continue to feel like this, the problem can go on and on, the hurting will not stop and peace will not come.

Forgiving someone who has hurt you is very difficult indeed. Forgiving does not mean saying that something terrible that was done was all right. Forgiving does not mean that what was done should not be punished and it does not mean forgetting about it. It means learning to live with that terrible thing without feeling hatred and anger. Some find it impossible to forgive but others find that forgiving is the only way their suffering can be "healed" and they can rebuild their shattered lives.

**ERIC LOMAX** was taken prisoner by the Japanese during the World War II. He and many others were forced to work in appalling conditions building a railway. It was a living hell: the men were starved and beaten and tortured and thousands died. Ever since this time, Eric could not lead a normal life. He was eaten up with anger and hatred and the desire for revenge. One Japanese man, in particular, he wanted to kill was the interpreter of his former interrogator.

Fifty years later he was, remarkably, able to track him down. Now was his chance. After some time they arranged a meeting. They met at Kanburi, the site of the prison camp. But his former torturer turned out to be in fact a very different man from the one Eric had thought him to be. Just as Eric had been suffering for all those years, so too had he. He had spent the years after the war trying to make amends for what he and his compatriots had done. As they talked and got to know each other they found that they had many things in common and they became good friends. Eric wrote: "Meeting Nagase has turned him from a hated enemy with whom friendship would have been unthinkable, into a blood brother . . . sometime the hating has to stop."

**ELIAS CHACOUR** was seven years old when, in 1947, some armed Jewish soldiers entered his village in northern Palestine. Elias' father told his children not to be afraid. He said, the soldiers had guns because they were afraid. They had suffered terrible persecution. They would not use the guns. However, they did. The soldiers took over the village and many others, killing many Palestinians. Those that survived fled for their lives. They have never been allowed back. They lost their homes, their land, their way of life. The newcomers changed the name Palestine to Israel.

In spite of all that has happened to him, his family and fellow Palestinians, Elias Chacour, who has become a priest, spends his life trying to build bridges between Jews and Palestinians. He is a very busy man setting up schools and libraries, community centres and youth clubs. He helps Palestinian students visit Jewish kibbutzim and Jewish students to live for short periods in Palestinian villages. He says: "If we cannot live together, we will surely be buried here together."

# Coventry Cathedral

On the night of Thursday, 14th November 1940, the beautiful mediaeval cathedral at Coventry was bombed by the Germans. The main part of the cathedral was destroyed; amazingly the tall spire survived. The very next morning the provost of the cathedral picked up two burnt roof timbers that he found lying in the form of a cross. He placed them against the blackened wall and wrote the words "Father forgive." From that time on

the cathedral has become a focal point of reconciliation and international exchanges. A new modern cathedral has been built beside the ruins of the old one.

Coventry Cathedral

During and after the World War II, pacifists worked in dangerous circumstances to help all victims of the war irrespective of their nationality. For example groups of Quakers from the Friends Ambulance Unit went to Germany, the country we had been at war with. A nurse, Pip Turner, wrote: "The Germans had *nothing*: no bandages, no soap, nothing. I ended up in Bochum in the Ruhr. This was a desert of ruins with hardly anything standing. People were living underground in cellars." Pip and others like her did their best to organise help and supplies for all these people. She wrote: "There was mute 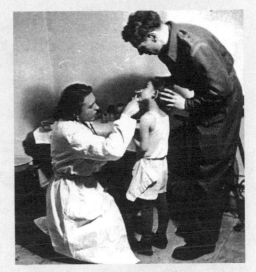 hostility when we first went into Germany but we soon overcame that. We went into many German homes and made good friends."

After the end of World War II, 25 women who had ugly and painful scars from their terrible burns at the time of the Hiroshima bomb, were brought to New York. There, surgeons performed many operations free-of-charge and US families looked after the women in their homes. Together these doctors and the families went some way to helping the wounds to heal so these women could smile a little again.

---

*It is better to light a candle than to curse the darkness.*
— Chinese proverb

*Goodbye War.* Painting by Nasime Gojayev, 13. He and his family were forced to flee their home in Nagorno Karabakh, Azerbaijan in 1991.

# Alternatives to War

Disputes are bound to arise from time to time between nations just as they do within families or between neighbours. It is not considered acceptable for neighbours to fight each other to solve a problem by force. If necessary they will go to court to seek a solution. It is also possible for nations to go to court. The court is called the "International Court of Justice" or World Court and it is in the Hague in the Netherlands. The World Court is an important part of the United Nations.

## The United Nations

The United Nations organisation was set up in 1945, after World War II, with the aim of keeping international peace and security. It is based in a big building in New York City and each country contributes money to pay for it and has members who form a General Assembly. Today 191 countries belong to the United Nations. There is a Security Council with five permanent members—China, France, Russia, the United Kingdom and the United States—and ten other members elected by the General Assembly.

The United Nations is very important because it is a place where representatives of different countries can meet and talk to each other. Through talking, agreements about difficult problems can be reached.

When fighting breaks out the Security Council may be able to arrange a ceasefire. Then UN peacekeepers may be sent in to make sure that the opposing sides do not start fighting again. The United Nations does not have an army—the soldiers come from the different countries that make up the United Nations and when they are working for the UN observers carry no arms and wear blue berets (hats). During the 50 years from 1948–1998, the United Nations carried out 48 peace-keeping operations in different parts of the world.

The United Nations is involved in much other work. It provides help in rebuilding after war, care for refugees, supervision to make sure elections are carried out fairly, support in improving living conditions for the poor and so on.

The United Nations can only work well when the countries who are part of it want it to work well. By itself it can do nothing. To help it work well we must support it, improve it and strengthen it.

# Nonviolent Action

We can oppose things we believe to be wrong and try to bring change without killing or hurting people. Such actions are called "nonviolent." Nonviolence can take many different forms. It can be very dramatic and involve many people or can happen quietly and involve only a few.

**MAHATMA GANDHI** used nonviolence in the struggle to free India from British rule. During the struggle he organised a 240 mile march to the sea to protest the salt tax. The salt tax meant that Indians had to pay their British rulers for something that was essential to life. Volunteers were trained in nonviolence beforehand. At the sea they made their own salt which was against the law. Many people were arrested. After that they tried to take over a salt factory. Police struck them down with heavy sticks but they did not fight back. Eventually the British agreed to change the salt tax.

**MARTIN LUTHER KING, JR.** practised nonviolent resistance in the United States. African-American people suffered a great deal at the hands of white people and were not allowed into many places in towns and cities, for example, eating places and swimming pools. They had separate schools, colleges, buses, churches and hospitals. In some places blacks were

only allowed to sit at the back of the bus and had to give their place to a white person when the seats at the front were full. In 1963 in Birmingham, Alabama, Martin Luther King, Jr. helped organise a mass protest and demonstrations against this policy of separation called segregation. At first 250 volunteers attended training sessions in nonviolence. Thousands of people joined in the demonstration. The police tried to stop them and made many arrests. They beat the protesters with clubs and set their dogs on them. The police used high pressure water hoses which broke their bones but the people did not give up or fight back. Soon the prisons were full and President John F. Kennedy began to press the local white leaders of Birmingham to talk to the blacks. All the protesters demands were agreed to.

These actions took place in order to change things within India and within the United States without fighting. Nonviolent resistance has also been used to counter attacks by one country on another. Here are two examples.

# Norway 1940

Norway was invaded by Germany at the beginning of World War II. The Norwegians were not in a position to fight back. The king and members of the government escaped to England and the Germans took over the country. Although the Norwegians did not fight the Germans they resisted them in many other ways using their "hearts and brains." When the Germans ordered all teachers to join the Nazi teachers' association, 12,000 out of 14,000 teachers refused. They lost their jobs and hundreds were arrested and taken in unheated cattle trucks in freezing weather

'Intet kan hindre en stjerne a tindre' (Nothing can stop a star shining). The cover of this book shows a card smuggled out of Girni Concentration Camp in 1941.

to do dangerous work unloading bombs and bullets from boats in the frozen north. But they did not give in. After six months the Germans let them come home. The clergymen and those working for the church also refused to cooperate with the Nazis. When the Germans tried to take over and control the sports clubs, the sports men and women stopped taking part in any sports activities. Even school children took part in the resistance—when ordered to attend a Nazi youth exhibition, they simply stood staring at their shoes!

Many people were arrested and put in prison and in concentration camps. Many were shot. But the people continued to resist and to stand together. At one time they wore paper clips to symbolise to each other that they were "sticking together." A secret underground newspaper was circulated in spite of the danger of being caught. It was so successful that it was sometimes possible to inform and organise a protest event to take place at the same time all over the country. Part of the work of the resistance was to raise money for those who had lost their jobs and salaries and to arrange the escape of Jews and those in danger because they had helped Jews. They escaped over the border into Sweden.

## Czechoslovakia 1968

In 1968 the Russians invaded Czechoslovakia. The Czechs, realising the pointlessness of violent resistance, instead countered the invading forces with nonviolent resistance. They obstructed the movement of armies and equipment on the railways, removed road signs, blew up bridges, sat down in front of tanks, and explained their views to the invading soldiers. The soldiers became confused because they had been told they had come to 'liberate' the country. Due to these nonviolent actions which were spontaneous and unplanned, it took the Russians six months to take control of the country.

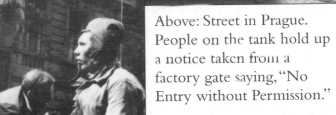

Above: Street in Prague. People on the tank hold up a notice taken from a factory gate saying, "No Entry without Permission."

Left: Ordinary people of Prague talking to Russian soldiers.

25

# France 1970

Throughout the 1970s (1970–81) a nonviolent battle took place between French sheep farmers of the Larzac plateau in southern France, their government and the army. The government wanted to make a huge extension to an army training ground and this meant many farms and villages would disappear. They were only a community of sheep farmers. How could they defend themselves?

They began by meeting, talking and organising to rally support. They held a demonstration. In the meantime, the government announced its decision to go ahead. However support for the farmers was spreading within and outside the region. Lanza del Vasto, a Catholic follower of Gandhi, helped them to feel the importance of remaining strong and, above all, united: 103 signed a pledge never to sell their land to the army. It became known as the "Manifesto of the 103."

The farmers were very successful in gaining wide publicity for their struggle: in February 1972 workers in the nearby town demonstrated their support by setting off the town's sirens while the farmers lit huge bonfires on the hills; the farmers travelled many miles in convoys of tractors meeting thousands of supporters on the way. They even took a flock of sheep to graze under the Eiffel Tower in Paris!

As the government took no notice and continued with the preparations for the planned extension, the farmers became more determined and began to resort to other means to save their land: they ploughed up and cultivated army land, they built new farm buildings without building permits, they dug channels and laid water pipes even when the police tried to stop them, they entered offices and destroyed land files, they set up a Land Trust to buy any land for sale to prevent the army from buying it, they intervened in army exercises, blockaded trucks and handed leaflets to soldiers, deflated the tyres of army trucks and painted slogans on them. On one occasion they towed away a gun with a tractor.

Many committees were set up all over France to support them and hundreds of volunteers took part in building and other activities. They forged links with other groups whose way of life was under threat: in 1974 100,000 people attended an event which included harvesting wheat for the starving in the African Sahel. They gained so much support that a new prime minister was elected in 1981 who cancelled the planned extension—it was total victory.

Not only did they save their land but their collective struggle brought many positive things: they continued to work together to improve their farms, develop renewable energy resources, build holiday centres for children and the disabled. They wanted Larzac to remain a centre for all those interested in peace and nonviolent change.

> *I would say I am a non-violent soldier. In place of weapons of violence, you have to use your mind, your heart, your sense of humour, every faculty available to you . . . because no one has the right to take the life of another human being.*
>
> — Joan Baez (American singer)

Nonviolent confrontation at the
Pentagon, Washington, D.C.,
October 21, 1967.

Tiananmen Square, Beijing, Peoples Republic of China, June 4, 1989.

28

# Opposing the War Machine

Conscientious objectors are men and women who refuse to take part in a particular war because they feel it is wrong. Pacifists are those who believe that it is always wrong to kill other people in any war. During World War II in Britain conscientious objectors were allowed to do alternative service which did not involve taking part in the war, e.g. working on the land. But in many countries conscientious objectors and pacifists who refuse to join the army during a war or to do their military service, may be imprisoned, severely punished or even shot.

**OSMAN MURAT ULKE** is a Turkish pacifist. He has been in and out of the prison since October 1996. Each time he is called into the army he refuses and each time he refuses he is sent to prison. When he is released he is called up again and again he refuses. There are many people like him in different countries.

Sometimes soldiers involved in a war refuse to fight. They may be thought of as cowards. But quite the opposite could be true. It takes great courage to go against what everyone around you is doing because you feel it is wrong.

This is what happened to **WILLIAM DOUGLAS HOME** (the brother of Alec Douglas Home, prime minister of Britain from 1963 to 1964). Toward the end of the war, the British were preparing to bomb the French port of Le Havre, part of which was occupied by the Germans. Knowing the attack was imminent, the German commander in Le Havre asked the British to allow the French people to leave before the bombing began. The British refused. When William Douglas Home heard about this he refused to obey orders from his commander. He was thrown out of the army in disgrace and sent to prison. 12,000 French people were killed in the bombing. After the bombing of Le Havre, the British planned their attack on Calais. By this time William Douglas Home had managed to tell a British newspaper what had happened. On this occasion the people were allowed to leave. William Douglas Home's brave decision had helped save many lives.

**VIC WILLIAMS** was a soldier in the British army at the time of the Gulf war against Iraq in 1991. He refused to fight and was put in prison. He said: "I thought the war was wrong and unnecessary, it came too soon and it was too harsh. I knew that millions and millions of people would suffer. A year of my life is a very small price to pay for being able to object actively to something that was wrong. I am not sorry for what I have done—it was right for me."

**MORDECHAI VANUNU** made his stand for peace in another way. He was a technician in a nuclear factory in Israel. As he was working there he realised that nuclear bombs were being made secretly in the factory. He managed to collect information and take some photos. Later, he stopped working in the factory and left Israel. He was not sure what to do with the material he had collected and was very troubled in his mind. Eventually, in 1986, he decided that what was happening in the factory was so wrong that the world should know about it. He gave his information to a British newspaper and it was published so that everyone knew that Israel was secretly making nuclear bombs. The Israeli leaders were very angry and they arranged for Vanunu to be kidnapped. It was only when Vanunu wrote on his hand and it was photographed through the car window on his way to trial, that the world learnt about his capture. He had been drugged and put in chains and taken back to Israel by boat and has been in prison ever since. He spent 12 years completely on his own all the time with no one to talk to in a tiny cell. Now, fortunately, he is allowed to mix with other prisoners.

# The Ploughshare Campaign

In January 1996 four women entered the factory at
Warton, near Liverpool, UK where a warplane had been built

and was about to be sold to the government of Indonesia. The
government of Indonesia is a very cruel government and had sent
their army to invade the island of East Timor killing many of the
people there. This plane would be used to continue the killing.

The women managed, surprisingly, to enter the cockpit of the plane
and with only hammers they damaged it very badly. In fact they did
£1.5 million worth of damage. As no one came to arrest them, they
themselves called the factory security personnel to tell them what they had done. But the
most surprising and important part of the story is that when
they came to trial after spending six months in prison, the
jury decided they had not committed a crime. The women
succeeded in convincing the jury that their actions had been
taken in order to prevent a much greater crime: the killing
of innocent people. They were set free.

> *They shall beat their swords into ploughshares, and their spears into pruning hooks: nation
> shall not lift up sword against nation, neither shall they study war anymore.*
>
> — Isaiah, Chapter 2, Verse 4

## Greenham Common Women

For years a group of women camped outside the United States military base at Greenham Common near Newbury, UK where a type of nuclear weapons carried on 'cruise missiles' were kept ready for use. Their presence was a constant reminder of opposition to war and the desire of ordinary people to live in peace.

## Greenpeace

The environmental group, Greenpeace, began in 1971 as a protest against the testing of nuclear bombs in the United States. Campaigners protested and helped to awaken people about the dangers of what was being done by sailing their boats into the testing zone. In 1985 the Greenpeace ship, *Rainbow Warrior*, was bombed by French secret police when campaigners were protesting against the French nuclear tests in the Pacific.

The sunken *Rainbow Warrior* in Auckland harbour.

# The World Disarmament Campaign

In 1982 millions of signatures were collected from around the world to be presented at the United Nations Second Special Session on Disarmament. All these people signed their name to call on the governments of the world to get rid of their weapons and use the money spent in making them to end world poverty.

# The Peace Tax Campaign

We all pay money (taxes) to the government. Part of the money people earn goes to the government. Also, often, part of the price you pay for goods that you buy in the shops goes to the government. Those in government decide how to spend this money. A large part is spent on making weapons and preparing for war. Groups of people in different countries are working to persuade their governments to allow their taxes to be used instead to help prevent war and solve disputes in a peaceful way.

# International Peace Activists

Peace Brigades International (PBI) was founded in Canada in 1981 and now has projects in four countries. Volunteers accompany local people who are working for peace and human rights and are in danger either from their own government or other groups within their country. Sadly, as we see, for example, from the murder of Mahatma Gandhi and Martin Luther King, Jr., men and women of peace can be in great personal danger. The aim of the PBI volunteers is not to resolve conflicts themselves but to help local people work in safety so that they can bring about the necessary changes to build a peaceful and fair society.

In recent conflicts, for example, in Palestine and Iraq, groups of people from different countries have gone to the area to show their support for victims of violence and to be able to tell the world of their suffering.

## Aldermaston March

Nuclear bombs, invented in the 1940s, are so terrible that many millions of people have been drawn into the campaign to abolish them. In Britain nuclear weapons are made at Aldermaston. The first of the well-known Aldermaston ban-the-bomb marches took place in 1958. Over a period of several years this 50 mile march organised by the Campaign for Nuclear Disarmament (CND) became a regular event over the four days of Easter. Thousands of marchers took part—a few famous people and politicians but mostly ordinary people. Some with families, sometimes with babies in prams and even with their pets, singing together as they walked to take their minds off their aching legs and sore feet. Many spent the nights in schools and church halls on the way. The crowds swelled to tens of thousands at the final rally.

# Champions of Peace

Throughout history and throughout the world men and women have struggled against the forces of war and violence to bring change by peaceful means. Mahatma Gandhi and Martin Luther King, Jr. are well known. The following are a few more examples.

**MOTSE (468–401 B.C.),** a scholar in ancient China, lived in China 400 years before Christ and wrote about the power of universal love. He wrote: "When all the people in the world love one another, then the strong will not overpower the weak, the many will not oppress the few, the wealthy will not mock the poor, the honoured will not distain the humble, the cunning will not deceive the simple." He described various crimes ranging from stealing fruit from someone's orchard to the worst crime of murder which we all know to be wrong. He went on to say that if murdering one person is a crime then murdering a hundred people in a war must constitute a hundred crimes—and yet war and victory in war is praised. He said this is the same as a man who, seeing a little blackness says it is black, but when he sees a great deal of blackness says it is white! He said that whatever is gained in war never makes up for what is lost.

**WILLIAM PENN (1644–1718),** an English colonialist in American colonies, was a famous English Quaker. He founded the state of Pennsylvania where the capital, Philadelphia, means brotherly love. While he was the leader no one was allowed to carry arms. Penn sought to live in peace and harmony with the local Indians and in 1662 addressed them saying:

> The Great Spirit who made me and you, who rules the heavens and the earth, and who knows the innermost thoughts of men, knows that I and my friends have a hearty desire to live in peace and friendship with you, and to serve you to the utmost of our power. It is not our custom to use hostile weapons against our fellow creatures for which reason we have come unarmed.

**ALBERT LUTHULI (1898–1967),** an African tribal chief, was a black South African at a time when black South Africans suffered greatly at the hands of the white rulers. He came from the great warrior Zulu tribe. He became a brave and defiant leader. Although he struggled against white rule and was mistreated and imprisoned, he did not want to harm white people. He wanted everyone in South Africa, whatever the colour of their skin, to have equal rights and share in the running of the country.

**BADSHAH KHAN (1890–1988),** a nonviolent soldier of Islam, was also from a warrior tribe struggling against foreign rule. Whereas Albert was a Christian, Khan was a devout Muslim. A giant of a man standing 6 feet 6 inches tall, he came from the rugged mountain region of the North-West Frontier Province of British India part of which is now in Afghanistan and part in Pakistan. His people fought amongst themselves. Khan believed that their lives could be improved and foreign rule resisted only when they laid down their weapons. In 1929 he created the very first army of 100,000 trained nonviolent soldiers. They were called *Kudhai Khidmatgars* (Servants of God) or "Red Shirts" because of the colour of their uniforms. He told his army:

> I am going to give you such a weapon that the police and the army will not be able to stand against it. . . . That weapon is patience and righteousness. No power on earth can stand against it.

Badshah Khan was imprisoned many times both by the British and, later, the Pakistan government. In all he spent 30 years of his life in prison but he remained gentle and steadfast.

**JEANNETTE RANKIN (1880–1973),** a congresswoman from the United States, was a pacifist and the first woman to be elected to the US Congress. She spent much of her life campaigning for peace. She voted against United States entry into both world wars saying: "I want to stand by my country, but I cannot vote for war." At the age of 88 years she led 5,000 women on a march in Washington, D.C. to protest against the war in Vietnam. She wrote: "You can no more win a war than you can win an earthquake."

**CARL VON OSSIETZKY (1889–1938),** was a German journalist in Nazi Germany. After the horrors of World War I he joined the Peace Society. In 1926 he became editor of a magazine called *Die Weltbuhne* (*The World Stage*). He was not a mild, gentle man but intense and uncompromising and he used his pen fiercely to attack those who favoured violence. He wrote: "The hellish instruments of war must be smoked out while there is still time." In particular he wrote about the government's secret military activities and build up of arms. He spent many months in prison. He understood what type of man Hitler was and foresaw the rise of the Nazis. As the Nazis tightened their grip on the country Ossietzky continued to criticise the government and would not be silent. His friends urged him to leave the country to save himself but he refused. On February 27, 1933 the Nazis cracked down on all "enemies of the state" and

Ossietzky and many others were thrown into prison without trial. More than 50,000 people signed a petition asking for his freedom. He was so badly treated in a concentration camp that he never recovered and, five years later, died at the early age of 49 years. He was called an "outstanding hero of peace of our time" and awarded the Nobel Peace Prize in 1936.

**AUNG SAN SUU KYI (born 1945),** Burmese leader for justice and peace, is the daughter of Aung San who led Burma (now called Myanmar) toward independence from British rule but was assassinated when Suu was two years old. Suu studied at Oxford University in Britain and married an Englishman. In 1988 she returned to Burma to nurse her sick mother. It was a time of great unrest in the country as the army had seized power. Suu joined the campaign for democracy and human rights. In spite of the risks she spoke out fearlessly and when pressurised to leave the country she refused. She addressed hundreds of gatherings. Then the government  put her under house arrest which meant that she was a prisoner in her own home with no contact with the outside world not even with her own family. After six years under house arrest she was allowed out but was constantly watched and could not move about freely. When she tried to leave the capital, Rangoon, her car was stopped by the police. She refused to turn back and stayed in her car for ten days with little food or water. She was again put under house arrest. Then, after another short period of freedom, she was arrested and imprisoned in a secret location in May 2003. She continues to believe in nonviolent struggle to bring justice and freedom to her people and has been called the Gandhi of Burma. In 1991 she was awarded the Nobel Peace Prize.

**MAIREAD CORRIGAN MAGUIRE (born 1944)** is an Irish housewife. Violent clashes between Catholics and Protestants and bombings in Northern Ireland have resulted in thousands of dead and injured since 1969. One of the many innocent people caught up by chance in the violence was Anne Maguire. In August 1976 she was seriously injured and three of her children were killed when a car ran into them in the street. The driver had attacked a British soldier and then been shot dead at the wheel as he sped away. This terrible event shocked the whole country. It spurred Anne's sister, Mairead, and others to overcome their silence and fear and speak out against the violence around them. Within a few weeks, in spite of threats and attacks against them, thousands of people had joined the marches for peace. The movement they called "Peace People" grew and grew. Inspired by Mairead's courage and determination the quiet work of bringing Catholics and Protestants together and laying the foundations of a peaceful society in Northern Ireland goes on.

# The Nobel Peace Prize

Alfred Nobel was a Swedish scientist who invented the powerful explosive dynamite. As a result of his invention he became a very rich man. But, toward the end of his life, he became very troubled about inventing something so destructive. In his will he stated that the profits from the investment of his money should be used to pay for five awards each year. One of these awards was to be given to the person or persons who had most advanced the cause of peace. The first awards were given in 1901.

It is interesting that several of the people who have received the award were, like Alfred Nobel, scientists who, earlier in their lives, had helped in the development of powerful weapons. Later they deeply regretted their involvement and worked hard to make the world a more peaceful place.

**ANDREI SAKHAROV** was a Russian scientist and has been called "father of the Soviet hydrogen bomb." Later he tried to prevent the testing of nuclear weapons and became a fierce critic of his government. In 1975 he received the Nobel Peace Prize but was banished from Moscow by his government and was forced to live in obscurity for seven years.

**LINUS PAULING** was a US scientist involved in developing weapons during World War II. After the war he worked tirelessly in the face of strong opposition and ridicule to bring about a ban on nuclear weapons testing.

Professor **JOSEPH ROTBLAT** is Polish by birth. During World War II, he worked in the United States on the Manhattan Project that led to the development of the atomic bomb. But after a little while he resigned. He was awarded the Nobel Peace Prize in 1995 for his part in trying to abolish nuclear weapons.

# Children Working for Peace

## Britain

Many toy guns, tanks, soldiers are available for children to play with. Here a little boy is making his toy gun into a toy for peace, a musical instrument.

## Columbia

We want to live in peace

Violence in Columbia effects everyone, especially poor children. In 1996 the Children's Movement for Peace organised millions of children to vote in a special election declaring their right to live in peace. In the run-up to the election, thousands of children across the country took part in marches and candle-lit processions, planted trees and handed in their war toys.

# Japan

Sadako Sasaki died from leukaemia as a result of the atomic bomb dropped on Hiroshima. Before she died, she folded 964 paper cranes. In Japan there is a legend that if you fold 1000 paper cranes your wish will be granted. Sadako's wish, expressed in a poem she wrote before she died was: "I will write peace on your wings and fly you all around the world." Sadako's friends formed the Folded Crane Club and started a national campaign that built a monument to remind the world of what war can do to the young.

# Peace Museums

There is a growing network of peace museums all over the world. There are also peace parks and peace monuments. The stories of peacemakers and peace movements of the past can help and inspire us in our efforts to build a peaceful society and work against violence in all its forms.

There is an exciting project to build an International Peace Centre in Britain in the city of Bradford. Already exhibitions, discussions, events and school projects are taking place. In Japan there is a peace museum called Grass Roots House. The aim of the museum is to help people become aware of what war is really like and the value of peace. The organisers believe that the destruction of nature is another type of war and they seek to help us find ways of living that are more in tune with the natural world.

# Peace Calendar

**AUGUST 6TH and AUGUST 9TH** are the days we remember the thousands who were killed by the atomic bombs dropped on Hiroshima and Nagasaki in Japan at the end of World War II. In many places lanterns are floated down the river in their memory.

In 1999 the United Nations declared **SEPTEMBER 21ST** as International Peace Day as part of the Decade of a Culture of Peace.

**OCTOBER 24TH** is United Nations Day. In 1945, on October 24th, the United Nations officially came into existence. It is marked throughout the world by events, meetings and exhibitions on the achievements and goals of the United Nations.

**NOVEMBER 11TH** is Remembrance Day. You will be familiar with the red poppies that are worn to remember the soldiers killed in the war. White poppies are worn to remember all the victims of war and the importance of working for peace.

**DECEMBER 1ST** is International Prisoners for Peace Day. On this day supporters are invited to send greetings cards to those in prison for conscientious objection to military service and for nonviolent action against preparations for war.

# Peace Prayer

The words of this prayer are based on a passage in the *Upanisada*, a Hindu scripture. They have been said by many people all over the world, people of all religions and of no religion. The idea of devoting one minute each day to this prayer came from a woman and was announced by Mother Teresa of Calcutta in the summer of 1981. The prayer is an expression of the belief that outward peace, a world without war, needs to be founded on inner peace in the hearts of everyone. Saying the prayer each day has given a feeling of hope and unity to many people.

PRAYER for PEACE

LEAD ME FROM DEATH to LIFE, from FALSEHOOD to TRUTH

LEAD ME FROM DESPAIR to HOPE, from FEAR to TRUST

LEAD ME FROM HATE to LOVE, from WAR to PEACE

LET PEACE FILL OUR HEART, OUR WORLD, OUR UNIVERSE...

PEACE • PEACE • PEACE

# Peace in Practice

## Mediation

A mediator is someone who comes "in the middle" of two or more people or groups of people who are having an argument.

A mediator does not lay any blame or say who is right or wrong and does not come up with the solution. He or she helps the sides to find a solution themselves. They can do this by:

**1** Encouraging both sides to agree to mediation and preparing the ground for this, for example, by fixing a time and place. The sessions take place in private and the mediator does not normally tell others about what takes place.

**2** Making sure that each side can speak to the other in turn without interruption. The mediator takes the 'heat' out of the situation by encouraging both sides to explain their position without abusing or accusing the other.

**3** Helping the sides to agree to the exact nature of the problem.

**4** Listening for any clues to a solution. The mediator will ask questions and may suggest solutions and the advantages and disadvantages of them. Sometimes he or she will suggest a step–by–step approach or work on solving the easiest part of the problem first.

**5** Mediators may use bargaining to come to a solution. One side agrees to do something for the other if the other side will do something in return.

**6** Once an agreement has been reached and the mediator thinks it is fair it is usually put in writing and signed. The mediator will check that the agreement is carried out.

There are schools where some of the children have been trained to act as mediators to help solve problems between school children and even between children and teachers.

Mediation does not always work. The sides may refuse to speak to each other. An intermediary may go between them talking to each in turn. This may lead to mediation or it could lead to arbitration. Arbitration is when an outside person decides on a solution.

## Some Forms Of Nonviolent Action

- **PROTEST AND PERSUASION**

  **Aim:** to express disagreement, to change opinions, to gain publicity.

  ❐ **Demonstration**

  ❐ **March**

  ❐ **Protest meeting**

*You have to train to be nonviolent just as a soldier trains to be violent.*
— Cesar Chavez (leader of the United Farmworkers Union in the United States)

- **NON-COOPERATION**

  **Aim:** to show strength of feeling, to interfere in the way things are running.

  ☐ **Boycott (to stop buying or using services of a group or company)**

  ☐ **Strike (refusal to work)**

  ☐ **Refusal (for example: to pay taxes, be conscripted to the army, carry an identity pass)**

- **INTERVENTION**
  **(also called direct action)**

  **Aim:** to stop the way things are running.

  ☐ **Occupations, for example, taking over a building**

  ☐ **Obstruction, for example, blockading road and rail**

  ☐ **Setting up alternative systems, for example, Gandhi's making salt from the sea**

*Nonviolent resistance is not a method for cowards.*
— Mahatma Gandhi

# Terrorism

## What is terrorism?

Terrorism is the use of violence and killing by a group of people in order to bring about some change in what the government is doing or to change the government itself. The target may be important buildings or individuals or places where people gather. The attacks are designed to cause shock and focus publicity on the terrorist's demands.

## September 11th 2001

September 11th 2001 (or 9/11 as it is called) is the day four passenger aircraft were hijacked by terrorists in the United States. Two planes were flown into the Twin Towers of the World Trade Center in New York City, one plane hit the Pentagon (US Ministry of Defence) in Washington, DC and the fourth plane crashed in a field in Pennsylvania. The Twin Towers collapsed and altogether about 3,500 people were killed.

Acts of terrorism and killings have happened and continue to happen in many parts of the world but they do not receive the huge amount of attention and level of outrage as this attack. This is because it happened in the United States which is a rich and powerful country not used to being attacked.

After September 11th, the US President, George W. Bush, launched a "war on terrorism." The start of this war was an attack on the country of Afghanistan where the terrorists were said to be based.

Some relatives of people who had been killed in the destruction of the Twin Towers called on President Bush not to go to war and expressed their protest against war saying it was not in their name. Phyllis and Orlando Rodriguez lost their son. They wrote to the President:

> Your response to this attack does not make us feel better about our son's death. It makes us feel worse. It makes us feel that our government is using our son's memory as a justification to cause suffering for other sons and parents in other lands.

They helped form an organisation called "Peaceful Tomorrows" to seek peaceful answers to terrorism so as to break the endless cycle of violence and revenge.

After the war on Afghanistan a group of relatives went to that country to show their sympathy and friendship towards the relatives of some of the 8,000 ordinary people (not soldiers) killed there by US bombing.

## What is the difference between terrorism and war?

War is carried out by governments and large groups while terrorism can be carried out by individuals and small groups. In general, wars are fought between opposing armies. Terrorist attacks are usually random, surprise attacks. Governments want us to believe that war is lawful and acceptable at certain times. Terrorism is not lawful. However many governments in different parts of the world, in particular the United States, secretly—and not so secretly—support terrorist groups with money and training. The famous terrorist leader Osama bin Laden was funded and trained by the US government.

Both war and terrorism are acts of violence in which people are killed and injured. We have already seen that, as in terrorism, in war also many men, women and children are killed who are not soldiers and did not threaten anyone. In Baghdad 1,500 women and children were killed in 1991 in a bomb shelter by an American 'smart' bomb.

In war people are not only killed in fighting and bombing but die through losing their homes and livelihoods and through hunger and disease. Unexploded bombs and mines may injure and kill people long after the war is over, and damage to the environment leading to death or ill health may last many years.

**Many people believe that in fact there is little difference between war and terrorism.**

However, a government can find it useful to give the name "terrorist" or supporter of terrorism to those it wants an excuse to attack. The threat of terrorism helps governments pass laws which give them more power and control over people's lives.

**How do we *really* get rid of terrorism?**

1. Treat it as a crime.

   Terrorism is a crime whoever it is carried out by and for whatever reason. Terrorists are criminals and should be brought before a court of law and tried for their crimes.

   Treating terrorism as a crime has three important advantages:

   • it is peaceful;

   • it does not continue the cycle of violence and revenge;

   • we are all against crime.

2. Find and deal with the causes of terrorism.

Often the problems that lead to terrorist acts have been going on for a long time. To find the causes of terrorism, we have first to ask what reasons terrorists give for the terrible things they do. Why do they not try to bring about change or to express themselves by peaceful means? Their reasons are usually:

- anger at oppression or injustice and hatred of those responsible;
- to shock the public and to put pressure on the government;
- desperation because their voice is not being heard or to publicise their cause.

Although all acts of terrorism are criminal, we may find that the reasons for these acts, for example oppression and injustice, are valid. We may find that there are things that can be done that would take away the reasons that lead to terrorism.

For example, Northern Ireland suffered from terrorism for many years. In order to help bring peace, attempts are being made by the British and Irish governments to set up a new government there in which the opposing sides work together and share power.

3. Stop war, stop terrorism.

If terrorism is to stop, governments too must stop killing. If it is wrong for terrorists to kill, so too is it wrong for governments to organise killing. There should be one law for all. The hatred and anger created by war help turn people into terrorists. If we bring an end to war, we will go a long way towards bringing an end to terrorism.

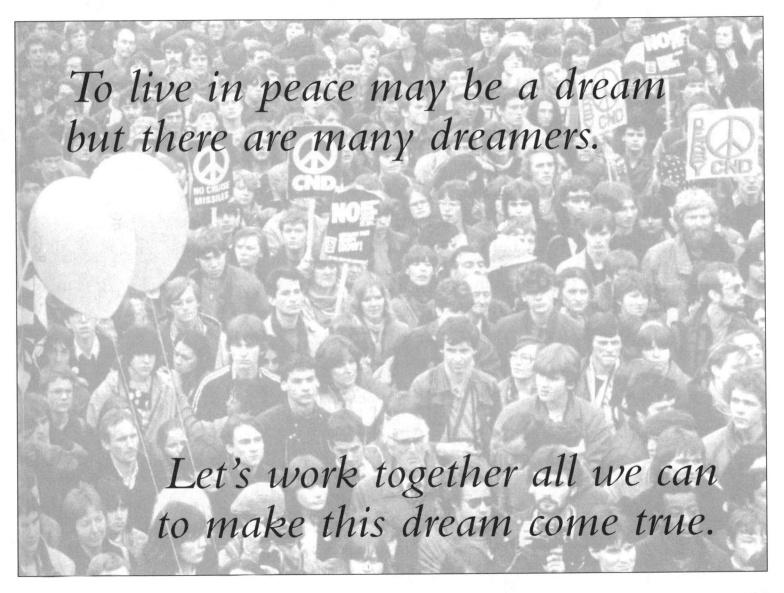

To live in peace may be a dream
but there are many dreamers.

Let's work together all we can
to make this dream come true.

# The Future

All over the world individuals and groups of people are working in different ways for peace. But we don't often hear about it in the news. Just as wars are made by people, they can be stopped by people. They do not have to happen.

We can all play our part in creating a world where there is no place for war.

Above all we have to have the courage and imagination to think of new ways of living together, of sharing the world and solving our problems without killing each other.

Sadly the beginning of the new millennium has brought yet more war and killing. It is more important than ever for us all to make time for peace.

*Ring out the thousand wars of old,*
*Ring in the thousand years of peace.*
— Alfred Lord Tennyson (English poet)

# Resources

**American Friends Service Committee (AFSC)**
1501 Cherry Street
Philadelphia, PA 19102, USA
*http://www.afsc.org/*

**Campaign Against the Arms Trade (CAAT)**
11 Goodwin Street
London N4 3HQ, UK
*http://www.caat.org.uk/*

**Campaign for Nuclear Disarmament (CND)**
162 Holloway Road
London N7 8DQ, UK
*http://www.cnduk.org/index.html*

**Council for Education in World Citizenship (CEWC)**
15 St Swithin's Lane
London EC4N 8AL, UK
*http://www.cewc.org/index.htm*

**Nonviolence.org**
*http://www.nonviolence.org/index.php*

**Pax Christi International**
St. Joseph's
Watford Way, Hendon    or
London NW4 4TY, UK
*http://www.paxchristi.net/*

532 West 8th Street
Erie, PA 16502-1343, USA
*www.paxchristiusa.org*

**The Peace Museum**
Jacob's Well
Manchester Road
Bradford, BD1 5RW, UK
*http://www.peacemuseum.org.uk/index1.html*

**Peace Pledge Union (PPU)**
41b Brecknock Road
London N7 OBT, UK
*http://www.ppu.org.uk/indexa.html*

**Quaker Peace and Service (QPS)**
Friends House, Euston Road
London NW1 2BJ, UK
*http://www.quakernet.org.uk/2001/in_advance/qps.htm*

**United Nations Association**
3 Whitehall Court
London SW1A 2EL, UK
*http://www.una-uk.org/*

**Women's International League for Peace and Freedom**
1312 Race Street
Philadelphia, PA 19107-1691, USA
*http://www.wilpf.org/*

**Woodcraft Folk**
13 Ritherdon Road
London SW17 8QE, UK
*http://www.poptel.org.uk/woodcraft/*

**Many other peace and justice organisations are listed in
*Housman's World Peace Diary and Directory*, 5 Caledonian Road, London N1 9DX, UK**

MARCH FROM LONDON TO ALDERMASTON

BAN THE BOMB